Ebbing & Growing

Ebbing
&
Growing

Chloë Robinson

Ebbing & Growing

Copyright © 2024 by Chloë Robinson.

All rights reserved. This book or any portion thereof may not be reproduced or used in any manner whatsoever without the express written permission except in the case of reprints in the context of reviews.

First published in Great Britain by Amazon Publishing

Cover Design by Chloë Robinson
Interior Designs by Chloë Robinson
Photography by Tom Lockwood

Paperback ISBN: 979-8-3252-4638-8

to my first love

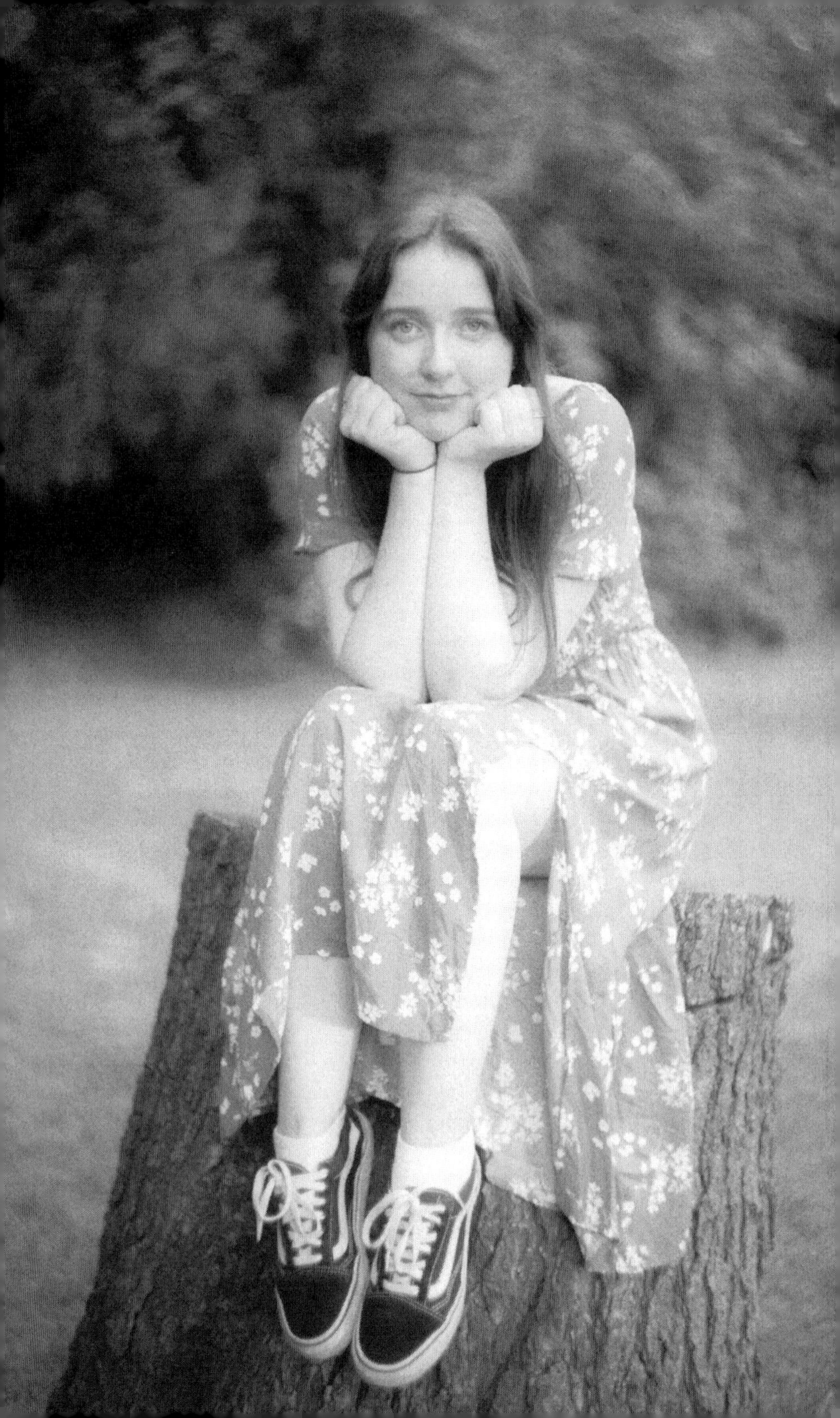

Acknowledgements

There aren't enough words to show my appreciation for the people that helped me in this project.

To the teachers who made me fall in love with words, and the teacher who made me fall in love with myself, Annemarie. My classmates and teachers at university who cultivated and nurtured each poem.

To the leaders at my church, St Philip's, who spoke words of wisdom over me. To Paul Ferguson and his infectious love for Jesus. To Jae Munro and his powerful love for poetry in his preaching.

To Tom Lockwood, my best friend, who not only did all the photography, but helped me design the pamphlet. Encouraged me in my writing, championed me, and responded to God's calling with me on this project.

To the Author, Perfecter, and Finisher, my Heavenly Father, for your sovereign hand and healing heart.

Thank you.

Contents

beloved III

I am searching for the one my heart loves IV

I.tend V

I.wavering VI

I.heal VII

joy VIII

How can a stone rise? XI

tefillah XII

II.waving XIII

II.tender XIV

II.healer XV

Κλίνω (Klinō) XVI

He is the Beginning...

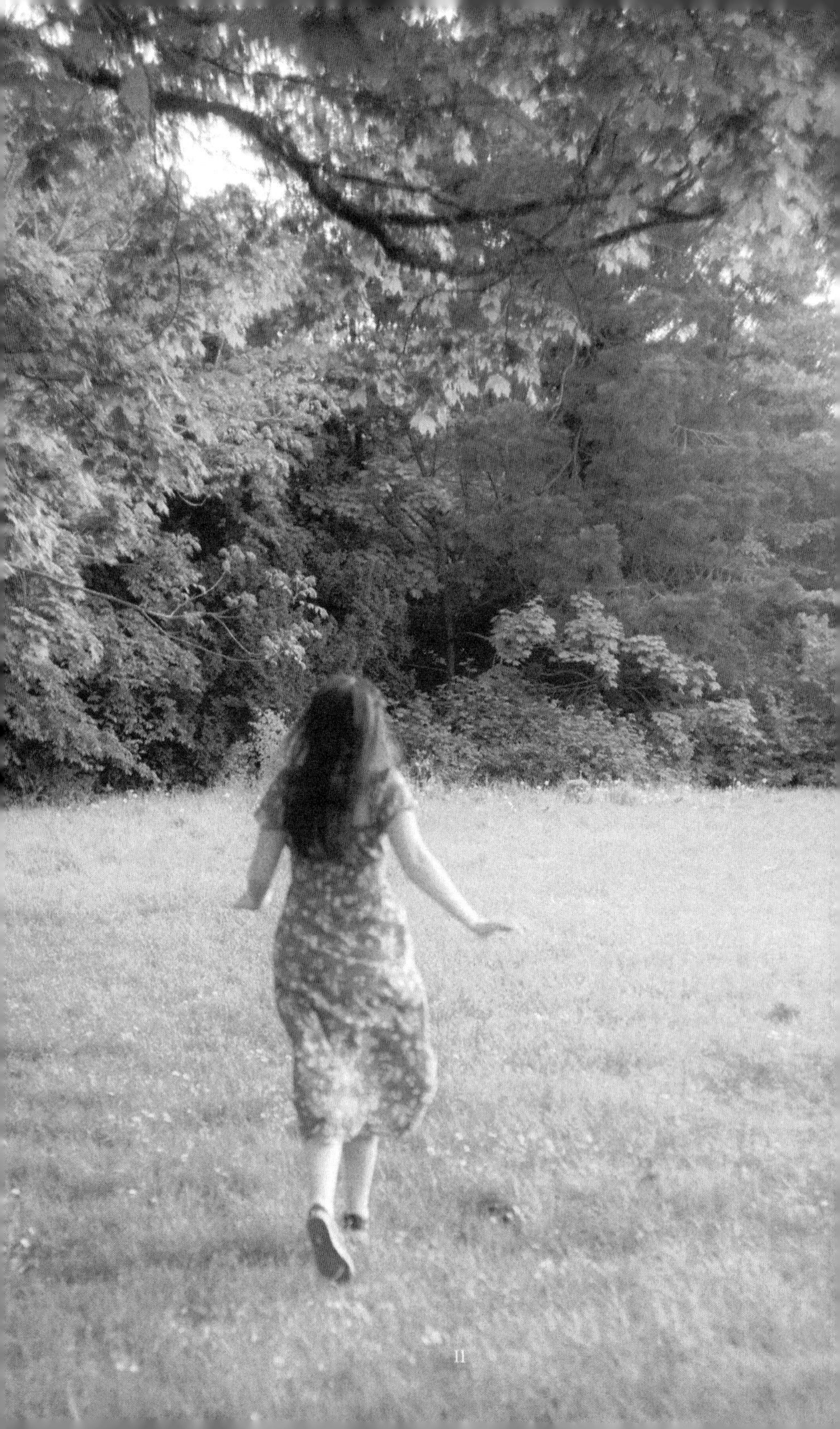

Beloved

Her
I want to walk with you in the cool of the day.
My beloved come to the garden and feast on my fruits.

                                        Him
                       You are a fountain in the garden.
              A deep well of flowing water, a spring of life.

Her
Call my name up in the mountains,
My beloved, meet me where the Heavens meet the earth.

                                        Him
                  You are still as a mountain in the valley,
          I will call on you, the same way I called you into being.

Her
I want to hear your voice in the morning,
My beloved, like a songbird, sweet melodies.

                                          He
                        You are my child, my own,
           My beloved, draw near and *I'll* sing of *your* beauty.

I am searching for the one my heart loves

The artist and the potter: Elohim Chayim.

To mend the fractured parts of me,

with the riches of His grace as the Kintsugi.

Allow me to break open the alabaster, as in Bethany.

To pour out the fragrance of my worship.

Soak your feet in my tears of joy,

for I will have found the one my heart loves.

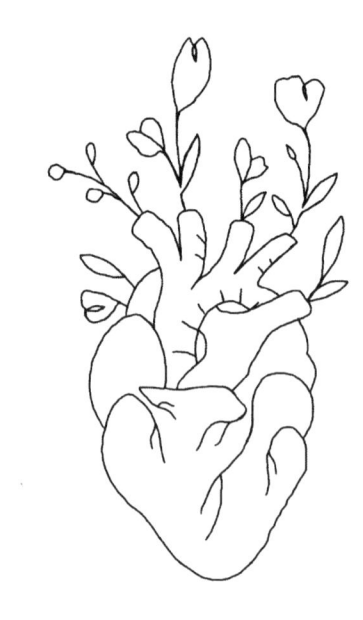

I.   **tend**

to the garden of my heart.
Cast vines, flora and fauna-

let wildflowers sprout from my aorta,
as it beats to the rhythm of yours.

Replace the withered willow,
cut away the dead, the barren and fruitless,

leaving behind the promise of primrose,
of new life and purpose.

Enter my inner chambers!
The gates are open wide for you-

there is nothing I wish to hide from you,
I pray, leave no stone unturned.

Inhabit my heart!
I'm making space, an upper room-

let it be the place your glory dwells,
where my faith swells in size.

Father, restore the fallows in me.
Tend to my soul like branches on a tree.

So that I might remain in you,

And **you in me.**

I. **wavering**

What can draw me from the boat?
    To leave the safety of my vessel and lean
not on my own understanding.
    How can I trust in the passing of the storm?
        When the waves bound at the boat
        like charging horses.
I step out into the unknown, and with my faith alone,
        I tread, deep in dread.
        Captured in the net of the sea, helpless as a herring.

    It's too late for faith.

        Why would you let me sink?

I.   **<u>heal</u>**

-As in Bethesda-

I will rest my faith
in the fountain.
Scramble and swim in search
of answers.
Return sodden and saddened;
Recumbent in sorrow.
Time after time meeting failure
face to face. I hide my face from you.
Forsaken and fraught;
I have naught to say to you.

So, I submerge my hope
in the fountain.

As the well of hope in you
runs dry.
Reposed in ruin.
Sinking as Babylon did.
Thirsting for a touch of those healing waters.
Those that cleanse and cure.
But I am forgotten and caught in the fray.
A minnow in a sea of sharks
fighting each day.

I have left my will in the fountain.

A maid laden with melancholy.
In the depths of acedia.

Father, I
beg that you will lift me
from grief like the mat from the pool.

joy

I didn't expect

that the light would come

and raise me from the dead.

That those wilted flowers

would be watered

and flourish.

For I heard no whisper

even in the silence

but sometimes He makes no sound;

I know this now.

For the light came

and I saw His face.

I have tasted freedom

once again.

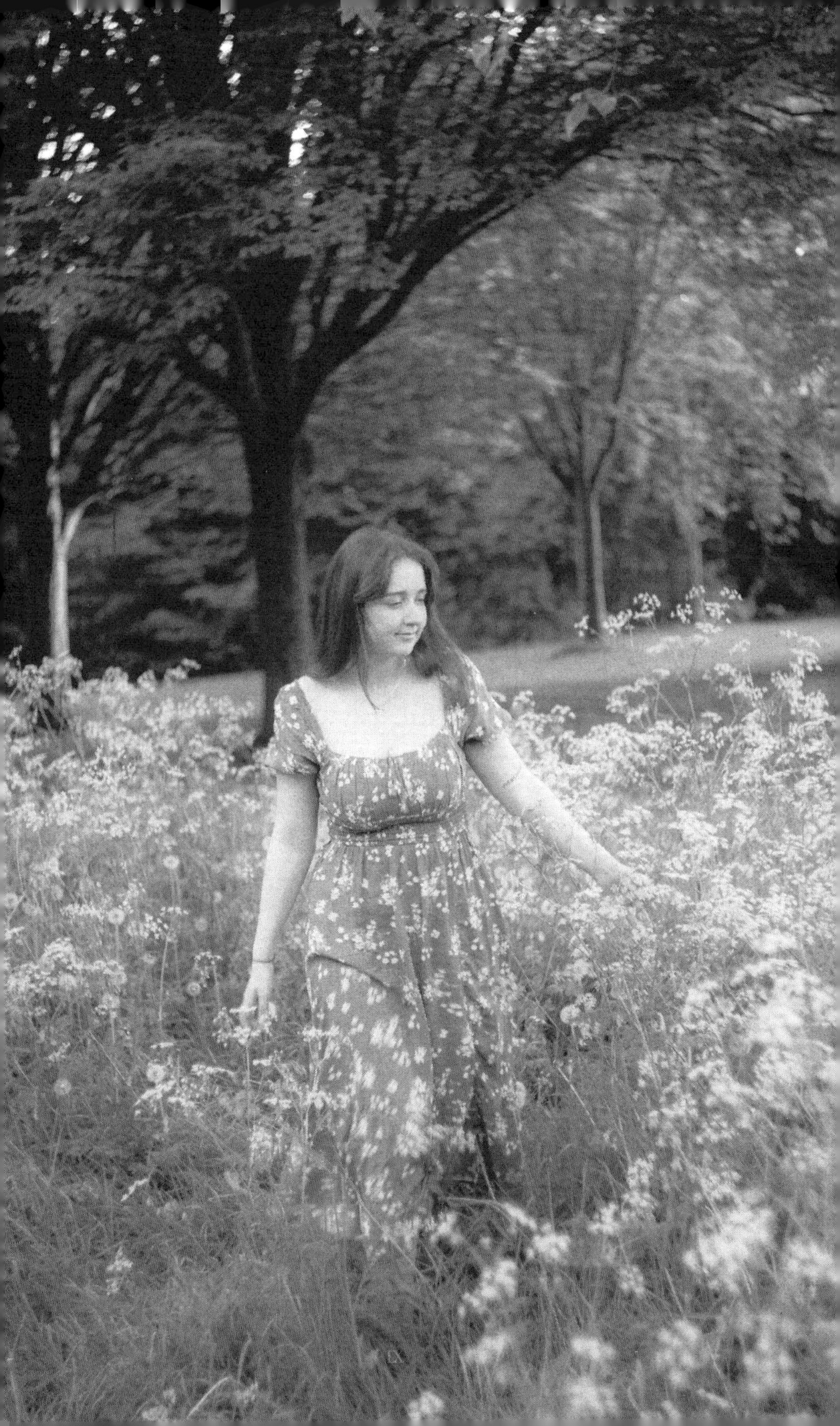

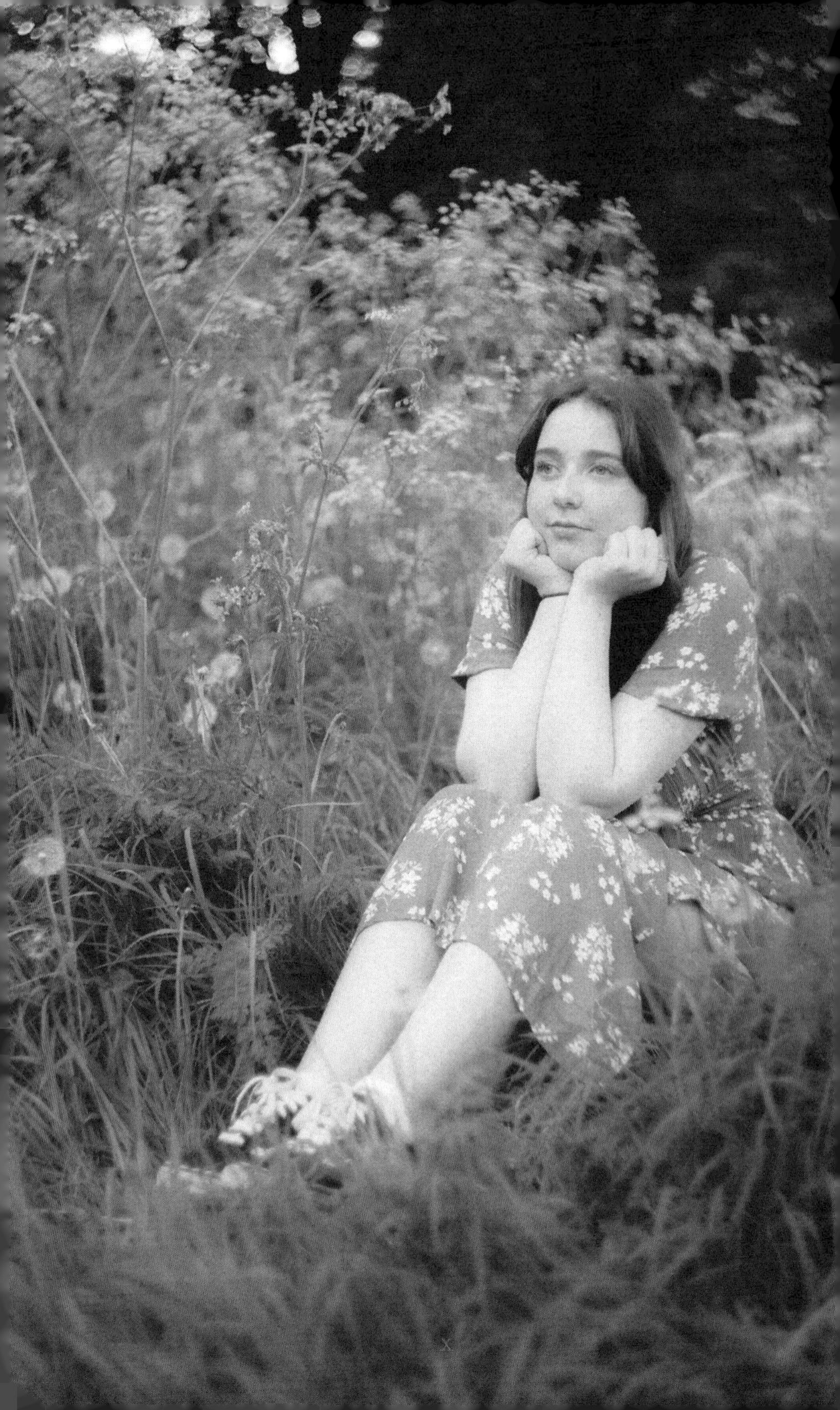

how can a stone rise?

Rising doesn't always mean going up.
But falling to your knees in reverence.
My child, bending takes force.
But bowing requires love.

How can a rock cry out?

My child, look up and posture your heart.
Hear the trumpets and listen to the joy of heaven.
Fill your lungs with praise;
Let your tongue only utter sweet words.

How can a stone be moved?

Only by faith can a mountain be moved.
A storm be silenced.
A dead man walk.
A nation, a people, a world,

    Be cleansed and set free.

tefillah

Father, why is this world so full of pain?

You are the God of justice, so why must it be this way?
I lay in the silence, and pray for the end of violence each day.

Don't you hear me cry out to you, arms stretched wide for you?

How long must you hide your face from me? Lord, just set me free.

I've been patient, waiting for the 'most ancient of days'.

How much longer must I wait,
before I can enter through the gates of heaven?

II. <u>**waving**</u>

Why did you doubt, my child?
Even when the seas grew wild, I was there.
There is to you, emunah.
Let your eyes not wander.
Walk on the water, don't let the fear make you falter.
You are my daughter.
I am strengthening you in your suffering, seek me first and

you will not sink.

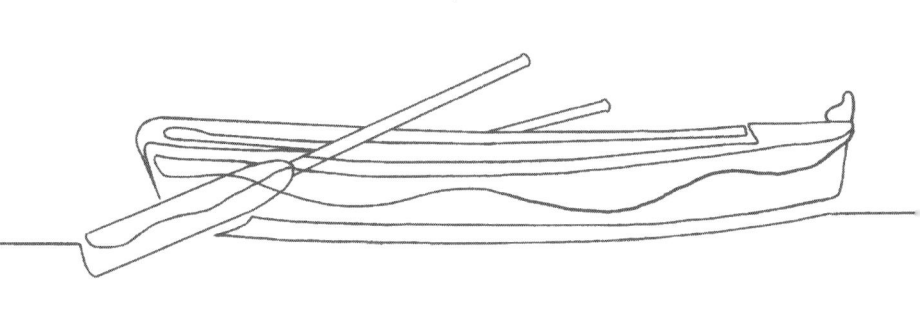

II. **tender**

is the voice that calls me deeper,

further into the forest.

In the whisper of the wind, you welcome me home.

My heart strives to sing softly in response.

But I, like a watering can,

cannot contain the praises. Cannot sit idly.

I shall not let the rocks cry out before I do.

Nor the fields shout with joy.

Instead, I will bow before the botanist of beauty

and let my soul

be still.

II. **<u>healer</u>**

While you weep my child

remember who you are.
Remember the strength within you.
You are fearfully and wonderfully made.

I did not create you by mistake.
Like a fountain of life, you will be renewed.

So shed those grave clothes,
for you're alive and well. Hell has no hold on you.

Bind yourself not with grief
but be set free by the promise of who you will be.

Your mourning will soon turn to dancing.

Child, I have not forgotten you.
It's only a matter of time.

Κλίυω

-Klinō-

Take me back to the garden.

Let me drink from your river of delight.

Let the fragrance of my worship be like petrichor in summer.

Worn like a sweet-smelling perfume.

My first love,

I'm waiting for your call.

Knock on the door of my heart,

And I will answer.

Chavah. Mother of all mankind,

You, her child.

I know you.

Return to me, teshuvah.

Return to what is good and right.

Return to the land of milk and honey.

To what is promised.

Rest.

XVII

...and He is the End.

About the Author

Chloë Robinson is a UK based poet. She is in her final year at Bath Spa University studying Creative Writing. Since childhood she has had a passion for poetry, and an equal love for praising the Lord. This is her first pamphlet, of which she hopes to be many.

Index

Elohim Chayim - (Hebrew)

Eh-lo-him Ha-yim

Elohim Chayim is translated into English as 'The living God' or as 'The God who is alive'.

Kintsugi - (Japanese)

Kin-tsu-gi

Roughly translated as 'joining with gold', Kintsugi is the art of repairing broken pottery with gold.

Bethesda - (Aramaic)

Beh-thes-duh

Loosley translated, Bethesda means house of mercy. The pool of Besthesda (which the poem references) was a location seen as a place of disgrace due to the presence of invalids, and as a place of grace due to the granting of healing.

Acedia - (Latin)

Uh-see-dee-uh

Defined as spiritual sloth. Primarily caused by a state of melancholia that leads to spiritual detachment rather than laziness.

Tefillah - (Hebrew)

Te-fee-luh

Tefillah is translated into English as 'prayer'.

Emunah - (Hebrew)

Eh-moo-nah

Emunah is translated into English as 'faith' but more precisely 'confidence' and 'trust'.

Chavah - (Hebrew)

Ha-vah

Chavah is a feminine name of Hebrew origin meaning 'life' or 'to give life'. It is the Hebrew form of Eve-the first woman created.

Teshuvah - (Hebrew)

Te-shoo-vah

Teshuvah simply means 'to return' and 'to repent'. As if returning to something you've strayed or looked away from.

Klinō - (Greek)

Klee-now

Roughly translated as 'laying down', 'to rest', 'to bow down', 'to bow ones head'.

Printed in Great Britain
by Amazon